D1088949

LET'S COMPOST!
CARING FOR OUR PLANET

By VITA JIMÉNEZ

Illustrations by GEORGE ERMOS

Music by MARK OBLINGER

CANTATA
LEARNING

WWW.CANTATALEARNING.COM

CANTATA
LEARNING

Published by Cantata Learning
1710 Roe Crest Drive
North Mankato, MN 56003
www.cantatalearning.com

A note to educators and librarians from the publisher: Cantata Learning has provided the following data to assist in book processing and suggested use of Cantata Learning product.

Publisher's Cataloging-in-Publication Data
Prepared by Librarian Consultant: Ann-Marie Begnaud
Library of Congress Control Number: 2016938059
    Let's Compost! : Caring for Our Planet
    Series: Me, My Friends, My Community
    By Vita Jiménez
    Illustrations by George Ermos
    Music by Mark Oblinger
    Summary: In this catchy song paired with colorful illustrations, children learn how to reduce, reuse, and recycle.
    ISBN: 978-1-63290-782-0 (library binding/CD)
Suggested Dewey and Subject Headings:
    Dewey: E 363.728
    LCSH Subject Headings: Organic wastes – Recycling – Juvenile literature. | Environmental responsibility – Juvenile literature.
| Organic wastes – Recycling – Songs and music – Texts. | Environmental responsibility – Songs and music – Texts. | Organic
wastes – Recycling – Juvenile sound recordings. | Environmental responsibility – Juvenile sound recordings.
    Sears Subject Headings: Compost. | Environmental protection. | School songbooks. | Children's songs. | Jazz music.
    BISAC Subject Headings: JUVENILE NONFICTION / Recycling & Green Living. | JUVENILE NONFICTION / Music
/ Songbooks. | JUVENILE NONFICTION / Science & Nature / Environmental Conservation & Protection.

Book design and art direction: Tim Palin Creative
Editorial direction: Flat Sole Studio
Music direction: Elizabeth Draper
Music written and produced by Mark Oblinger

Printed in the United States of America in North Mankato, Minnesota.
122016   0339CGS17

ACCESS THE MUSIC!

SCAN CODE WITH MOBILE APP

CANTATALEARNING.COM

TIPS TO SUPPORT LITERACY AT HOME

WHY READING AND SINGING WITH YOUR CHILD IS SO IMPORTANT

Daily reading with your child leads to increased academic achievement. Music and songs, specifically rhyming songs, are a fun and easy way to build early literacy and language development. Music skills correlate significantly with both phonological awareness and reading development. Singing helps build vocabulary and speech development. And reading and appreciating music together is a wonderful way to strengthen your relationship.

READ AND SING EVERY DAY!

TIPS FOR USING CANTATA LEARNING BOOKS AND SONGS DURING YOUR DAILY STORY TIME

1. As you sing and read, point out the different words on the page that rhyme. Suggest other words that rhyme.

2. Memorize simple rhymes such as Itsy Bitsy Spider and sing them together. This encourages comprehension skills and early literacy skills.

3. Use the questions in the back of each book to guide your singing and storytelling.

4. Read the included sheet music with your child while you listen to the song. How do the music notes correlate to the words of the song?

5. Sing along on the go and at home. Access music by scanning the QR code on each Cantata book, or by using the included CD. You can also stream or download the music for free to your computer, smartphone, or mobile device.

Devoting time to daily reading shows that you are available for your child. Together, you are building language, literacy, and listening skills.

Have fun reading and singing!

What can we do to reduce the amount of garbage going into landfills? We can **recycle** some of the trash and use it to start a **compost** pile. Over time, compost turns into dirt, which we can add to our gardens. The compost becomes food for our gardens, helping our plants to grow.

Now turn the page and sing along!

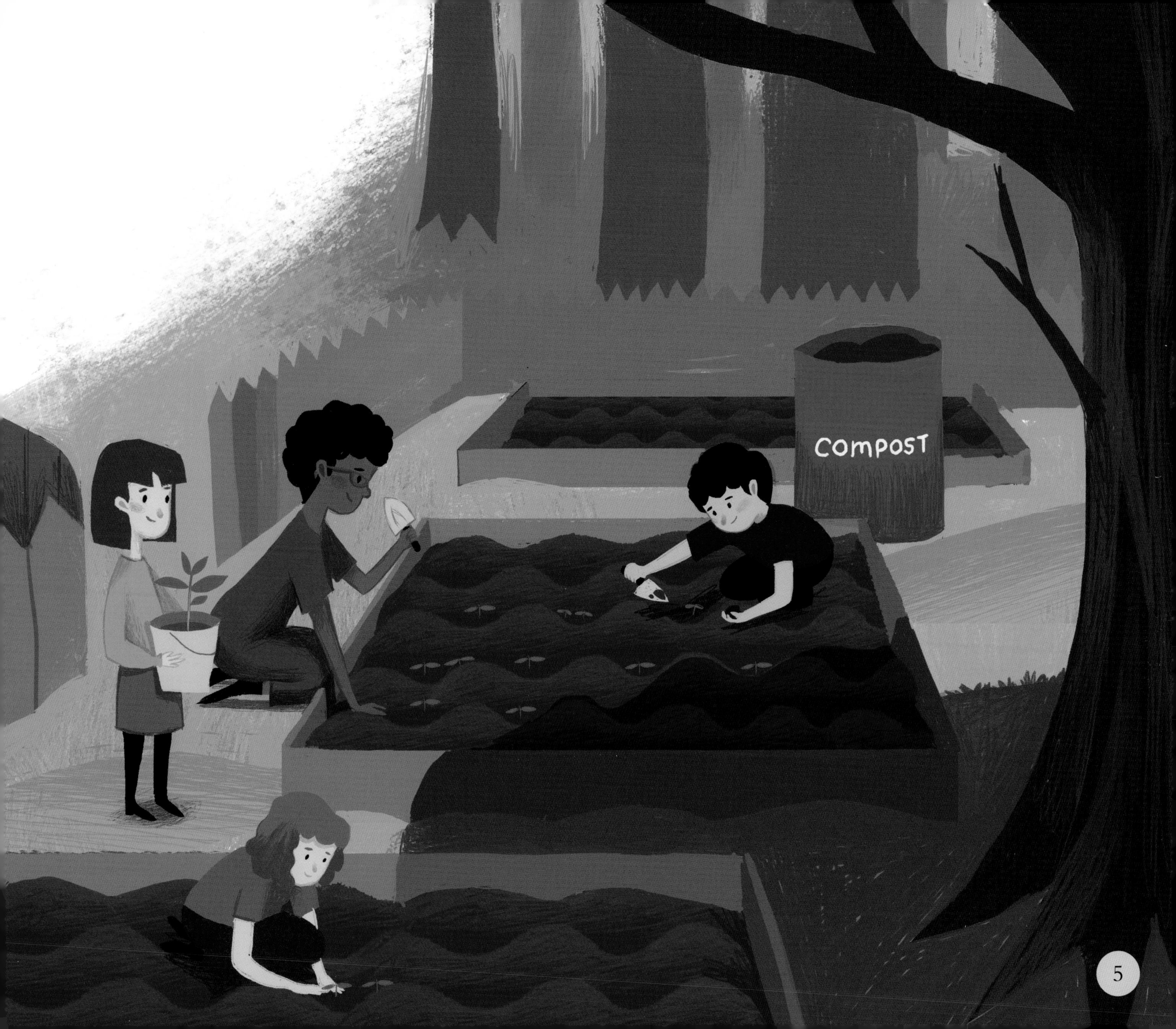
COMPOST

Compost raw fruit and veggies
at school or for your yard.

It's nature's way of recycling,
and it isn't very hard!

Separate trash to remove
glass, paper, plastic, and tin.

Separate food and yard waste,
and put them in a compost bin!

Compost raw fruit and veggies
at school or for your yard.

It's nature's way of recycling,
and it isn't very hard!

Newspaper, leaves, and grass,
fruit and vegetable skins,
these things are compostable.
Please put them in the bin.

Tiny **organisms**,
bacteria, fungi, and worms,
eat up all of the waste
and turn it into plant food.

Compost raw fruit and veggies
at school or for your yard.

It's nature's way of recycling,
and it isn't very hard!

Mix all the compost up,
add water, and give it some sun.

When its dark and **crumbly**,
then you'll know that it's all done!

The compost is ready to go
when it's dark, damp, rich, and brown.

Use a shovel to spread it
evenly on the ground.

Compost every day at school.
Don't throw all that food away.

Compost things like banana peels,
and make plant food nature's way!

Compost raw fruit and veggies
at school or for your yard.

It's nature's way of recycling,
and it isn't very hard!

Compost raw fruit and veggies
at school or for your yard.

It's nature's way of recycling,
and it isn't very hard!

SONG LYRICS
Let's Compost!

Compost raw fruit and veggies
at school or for your yard.
It's nature's way of recycling,
and it isn't very hard!

Separate trash to remove
glass, paper, plastic, and tin.
Separate food and yard waste,
and put them in a compost bin!

Compost raw fruit and veggies
at school or for your yard.
It's nature's way of recycling,
and it isn't very hard!

Newspaper, leaves, and grass,
fruit and vegetable skins,
these things are compostable.
Please put them in the bin.

Tiny organisms,
bacteria, fungi, and worms
eat up all of the waste
and turn it into plant food.

Compost raw fruit and veggies
at school or for your yard.
It's nature's way of recycling,
and it isn't very hard!

Mix all the compost up,
add water, and give it some sun.
When it's dark and crumbly,
then you'll know that it's all done!

The compost is ready to go
when it's dark, damp, rich, and brown.
Use a shovel to spread it
evenly on the ground.

Compost every day at school.
Don't throw all that food away.
Compost things like banana peels,
and make plant food nature's way!

Compost raw fruit and veggies
at school or for your yard.
It's nature's way of recycling,
and it isn't very hard!

Compost raw fruit and veggies
at school or for your yard.
It's nature's way of recycling,
and it isn't very hard!

Let's Compost!

Rock and Roll
Mark Oblinger

Chorus

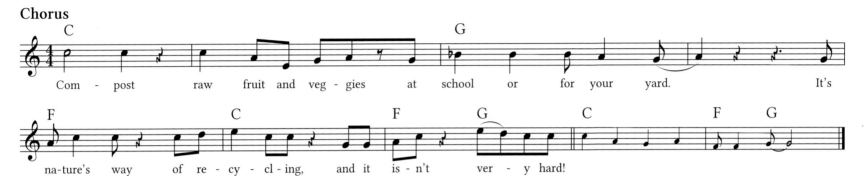

Com - post raw fruit and veg - gies at school or for your yard. It's
na-ture's way of re - cy - cl - ing, and it is - n't ver - y hard!

Verse

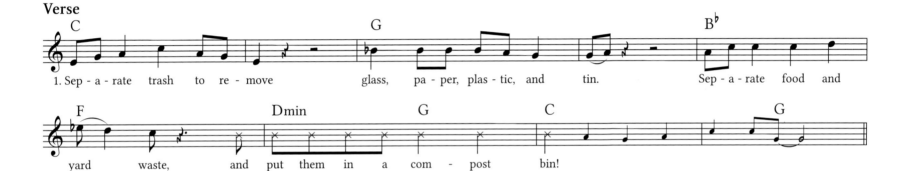

1. Sep - a - rate trash to re - move glass, pa - per, plas - tic, and tin. Sep - a - rate food and
yard waste, and put them in a com - post bin!

Chorus

Verse 2
Newspaper, leaves, and grass,
fruit and vegetable skins,
these things are compostable.
Please put them in the bin.

Verse 3
Tiny organisms,
bacteria, fungi, and worms
eat up all of the waste
and turn it into plant food.

Chorus

Verse 4
Mix all the compost up,
add water, and give it some sun.
When it's dark and crumbly,
then you'll know that it's all done!

Verse 5
The compost is ready to go
when it's dark, damp, rich, and brown.
Use a shovel to spread it
evenly on the ground.

Verse 6
Compost every day at school.
Don't throw all that food away.
Compost things like banana peels,
and make plant food nature's way!

Chorus (x2)

23

GLOSSARY

compost—a mixture of waste materials that can be used to make soil healthy

crumbly—easily breaking into small pieces

organisms—living things

recycle—to process something so that it can be used again

separate—to set or keep apart

GUIDED READING ACTIVITIES

1. Why do you think the writer chose this topic to write about?

2. Think of all the things that you threw in the garbage today. What things could you compost instead? Would you create less trash if you composted?

3. Would you keep a compost pile in your backyard? Why or why not?

TO LEARN MORE

Lay, Richard. *A Green Kid's Guide to Composting*. Minneapolis: Magic Wagon, 2013.

Porter, Esther. *What's Sprouting in My Trash? A Book about Composting*. North Mankato, MN: Capstone, 2013.

Rake, Jody. *Grubs, Bugs, and Worms: Invertebrates of the Underground*. North Mankato, MN: Capstone, 2016.

Schuh, Mari. *Compost Basics*. Mankato, MN: Capstone, 2012.